REPTILES

Written and Illustrated by Beverly Armstrong

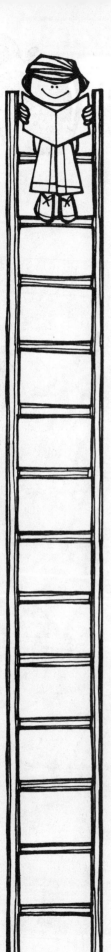

The Learning Works

Edited by Sherri M. Butterfield

The purchase of this book entitles the individual classroom teacher to reproduce copies for use in the classroom.

The reproduction of any part for an entire school or school system or for commercial use is strictly prohibited.

No form of this work may be reproduced or transmitted or recorded without written permission from the publisher.

Contents

Ball Python

The ball python lives in the dry forests and grasslands of central and western Africa. This shy, gentle snake is smaller than most other pythons, seldom exceeding six feet in length. When frightened, this python rolls itself into a tight ball with its head hidden inside. The ball python feeds mainly on mice and rats. To catch these rodents, it drapes itself over tree branches and remains almost motionless until one of them passes by. The ball python is most active at dusk, and has eyes with catlike vertical pupils that can adjust for daytime or night-time vision. Like other pythons, this snake lays eggs and is non-poisonous.

Coloring Clues

The ball python is beautifully marked with irregular patches of chocolate brown and golden yellow.

Activity Safari

1. The pythons of Africa, Asia, and Australia are related to the boas of North, Central, and South America. Do some research to learn about one of the snakes listed below.

blood python	rainbow boa
boa constrictor	reticulated python
green tree python	rock python
Indian python	rosy boa

   rubber boa

2. Many snakes are marked with beautiful colors and interesting shapes. First, look at pictures of snakes in a reptile book or an encyclopedia. Then, design a T-shirt based on the coloration and markings of one snake.

REPTILES © 1988—The Learning Works, Inc.

Ball Python (*Python regius*)

Basilisk Lizard

The basilisk lizard lives near streams and rivers in South American rain forests. This lizard has an amazing ability to "walk on water." By spreading its long, fringed toes and moving quickly, the basilisk can run along the water's surface, thus escaping both land and water predators. Small basilisks can travel more than a hundred feet in this manner. These lizards can also swim well. Basilisk lizards feed on small birds, insects, plants, and rodents. Adults may reach a length of thirty inches. When the female is ready to lay eggs, she digs a hole in the ground. In this hole, she deposits about twenty eggs, which she then covers with leaves and dirt. Three months later, the three-inch babies emerge. Like most reptiles, they may never know their parents.

Coloring Clues

The golden-eyed basilisk has a bright green body. Large specimens may be sprinkled with black and blue-green markings.

Activity Safari

1. The basilisk was a mythical monster. Look up this word in a dictionary or an encyclopedia and find out how a basilisk killed its enemies.

2. Basilisk lizard eggs take about ninety days to hatch. If a lizard laid eggs today, on what date would they probably hatch?

3. This lizard is sometimes called the "tetetereche" because of the sound that it makes as it runs across water. If each one of the animals listed below was named for the sound that it makes, what might it be called?

cat	goose
donkey	lion
frog	mouse
goat	pig

Basilisk Lizard (*Basiliscus plumifrons*)

Corn Snake

Corn snakes live in a variety of habitats in the eastern United States. They are especially common around farms and in fields, where they can find plenty of mice and rats to eat. These snakes are gentle and harmless to people. When startled, they sometimes vibrate their tails. In dry grass or leaves, this movement may produce sounds that resemble those of a rattlesnake. Adult corn snakes are about six feet long. They are related to chicken, fox, and rat snakes. All of these snakes destroy large numbers of harmful rodents and should be protected.

Coloring Clues

The corn snake's yellow-orange body is marked with red-orange or brown spots. Parts of its face and belly are white.

Activity Safari

1. Are chicken, corn, fox, or rat snakes found in the state where you live? Find out by consulting a book about reptiles in the United States.

2. In the springtime, corn snakes are **diurnal.** During the rest of the year, they are **nocturnal.** First, look up these words in a dictionary and learn what they mean. Then, tell whether you would rather be a diurnal animal or a nocturnal one and why.

3. A snake's incubation period is the length of time between the laying and the hatching of its eggs. Make a graph comparing the incubation periods of these snakes. The numbers indicate months.

corn snake	2	indigo snake	3½
grass snake	1½	reticulated python	5½
Indian cobra	2½	rock python	3

REPTILES © 1988—The Learning Works, Inc.

Corn Snake (*Elaphe guttata*)

Eastern Box Turtle

This turtle and its counterpart, the western box turtle, are found in fields and forests in many parts of the United States. They like to live near water, but not in it. Box turtles are omnivorous, eating such things as berries, cactus, mushrooms, snails, and worms. They hibernate in winter and may burrow underground in hot weather.

These four-to-eight-inch turtles are protected by their shells, which are hinged underneath. This shell can be pulled shut to form a tightly closed "box," with the turtle's head, legs, and tail inside.

Coloring Clues

The eastern box turtle's shell has yellow markings. The spots and scales on its face and legs may be orange, yellow, and/or white. Male box turtles have red-orange eyes; female box turtles have brown eyes.

Activity Safari

1. Box turtles often live for eighty years or longer. On what day, month, and year will you be eighty years old?

2. If undisturbed, a box turtle will probably spend its entire lifetime in an area two or three acres in size. How large is an **acre**? Use a dictionary to find out.

3. A box turtle is protected by its shell. Other animals defend themselves in a variety of ways. Think of at least one animal that is protected by each of the devices or defends itself in each of the ways listed below.

claws	size and strength	spines
coloration	smell	sting
poison	speed	teeth

Eastern Box Turtle (*Terrapene carolina*)

Gaboon Viper

The fat, sluggish gaboon viper lives in the forests of tropical Africa. A five-foot specimen may weigh almost eighteen pounds and have fangs that are more than an inch long. Four drops of its highly toxic venom can kill a man. As with all other poisonous reptiles, this venom is actually a very strong saliva that helps break down the snake's prey for digestion. Fortunately, the gaboon viper is not aggressive, and will bite a person only if provoked. It feeds on birds, rodents, and larger animals, including mongooses and warthogs.

Gaboon vipers mate between October and December. The young are born four months later. There may be more than fifty in a litter. These babies are eight inches long and are able to fend for themselves. They shed their skins shortly after birth and then go looking for food.

Coloring Clues

The gaboon viper is marked in shades of brown, tan, and cream.

Activity Safari

1. If a gaboon viper gave birth to forty-eight eight-inch babies, what would the total length of the litter be?

2. This snake's markings help to camouflage it among the leaves on the forest floor. Make a copy of this illustration and color it. Then cut out the snake and nestle it among dry, dead leaves near a bush or tree. How well does it hide?

3. The rhinoceros viper, a relative of the gaboon viper, is more brightly colored and has spikes on its nose. Find a picture of this snake in an encyclopedia or a reptile book.

Gaboon Viper (*Bitis gabonica*)

Galapagos Tortoise

These giant tortoises are found on the Galapagos Islands, two hundred miles from the coast of Ecuador. The adults range in length from thirty inches to four feet. Galapagos tortoises eat plants and wander to highland springs to drink water and wallow in mud. Originally, there were no predators on these islands, and the tortoises flourished. Then, in the eighteenth century, whalers and sea-going explorers discovered the islands and took thousands of tortoises onto their ships to eat. They also brought goats, pigs, and rats to the islands. These animals ate the tortoises' eggs and competed with them for food. Galapagos tortoises are now endangered and are protected on the islands.

Coloring Clues

Galapagos tortoises are dark gray or dusty tan.

Activity Safari

1. When explorers first arrived at the Galapagos Islands, tortoises with shells three feet wide and five feet long were common. To see how big these animals were, tape sheets of newspaper together to form a three-foot-by-five-foot rectangle.

2. In 1831, a young, excited scientist named Charles Darwin arrived at the Galapagos Islands. He was making a round-the-world voyage on a ship called the *Beagle*. Read about Darwin's adventures in his book, *The Voyage of the* Beagle.

3. The Spanish word **galapagos** means "tortoises," so these reptiles live on the "Tortoise Islands." Look at a map of your state to see if you can find places that have been named after animals, such as Otter Tail Lake (in Minnesota), Owl City (in Tennessee), and the Vulture Mountains (in Arizona).

Galapagos Tortoise (*Geochelone elephantopus*)

Green Turtle

Second largest of the sea turtles, the green turtle may have a four-foot-long shell and weigh as much as 350 pounds. This reptile is a strong, graceful swimmer with paddlelike legs and a streamlined shell. To go from the shallow waters where green turtles feed on sea grass to the distant beaches where they lay their eggs, these reptiles must travel through more than a thousand miles of open ocean.

Once common, green turtles are now endangered. People have hunted these beautiful animals for meat and collected their eggs for food. Hotels line many of the beaches where they once came ashore to nest. Like many marine animals, green turtles are adversely affected by pollution. If not protected, these reptiles may soon become extinct.

Coloring Clues

The green turtle's name refers to the greenish color of its flesh and fat. Its shell is a rich reddish brown. The dark brown scales of its body are separated by lines of white skin.

Activity Safari

1. The green turtle may use its keen sense of smell to find its way across the ocean. Are there places that you can identify by their smells? Describe some of the scents that might be found at a campground or park, in the stores of a shopping center, or at a carnival, circus, or fair.

2. Design a poster to be put on beaches where green turtles nest, warning people not to bother these endangered animals or their eggs.

3. Use an encyclopedia or a book about turtles to learn about the four other species of sea turtle: leatherback, loggerhead, hawksbill, and ridley.

Green Turtle (*Chelonia mydas*)

Indian Cobra

When excited or frightened, the Indian cobra sweeps its head upward, spreading its hood. Other animals are often scared away by the sudden appearance of the hood's eyelike markings. If provoked further, this six-foot snake may hiss and strike. The cobra has short, grooved fangs with which it hangs onto its victim while squeezing venom into the wound. This venom affects the central nervous system and may cause death by suffocation or heart failure. Indian cobras eat birds, frogs, rodents, and toads. In India, these reptiles are used for entertainment by snake charmers, who may pull the snakes' fangs or fasten their mouths shut to protect themselves.

Coloring Clues

The Indian cobra's body is marked with reddish brown and tan. The "eye spot" markings on the back of the hood are black and white. There are also black and white spots on the underside of the hood.

Activity Safari

1. The Indian cobra's range extends from Iran east to China. It is also found on the islands of Indonesia and in the Philippines. Locate each one of these countries on a map.

2. Cobras kill up to ten thousand people each year in India alone. Compare this figure with the population of the town or city in which you live. Is it smaller, larger, or just about the same?

3. The largest venomous snake is the king cobra, which may be twenty feet long. Cut a piece of string this length and stretch it out to see how long a king cobra is.

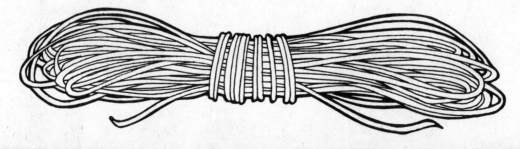

Indian Cobra (*Naja naja*)

Jackson's Chameleon

The four-inch-long Jackson's chameleon looks like a tiny dinosaur, climbing carefully along a twig with its strange grasping feet. One eye may scan the sky overhead for hungry birds while the other eye focuses forward on a fly. The thin, sticky tongue, held in this lizard's mouth like a compressed spring, can suddenly shoot out several inches to snag an insect. Even day-old babies catch their food in this way with amazing accuracy.

Chameleons are known for their ability to change color. They fade at night, and turn dark brown or black when angry or afraid. If part of the body is in sunlight and part in shadow, the shaded area will be lighter.

Coloring Clues

According to its mood and temperature, this chameleon may be marked with light or dark green, yellow, gray, brown, and/or black. The horns are brown.

Activity Safari

1. The chameleon has a prehensile tail. Elephants' trunks, giraffes' tongues, and monkeys' tails are also prehensile. If you do not know what the word **prehensile** means, look it up in a dictionary.

2. Chameleons stake out and guard territories which contain the food, shelter, and water that they need. If you had to stake out a territory to live in, what would you want it to contain? Draw a map of the territory you would like to claim.

3. When fully extended, this chameleon's tongue can be as long as six inches. Imagine that, for twenty-four hours, you could have a chameleon-style tongue that was one and one-half times the length of your body. Write a story about the things you would do with your amazing tongue.

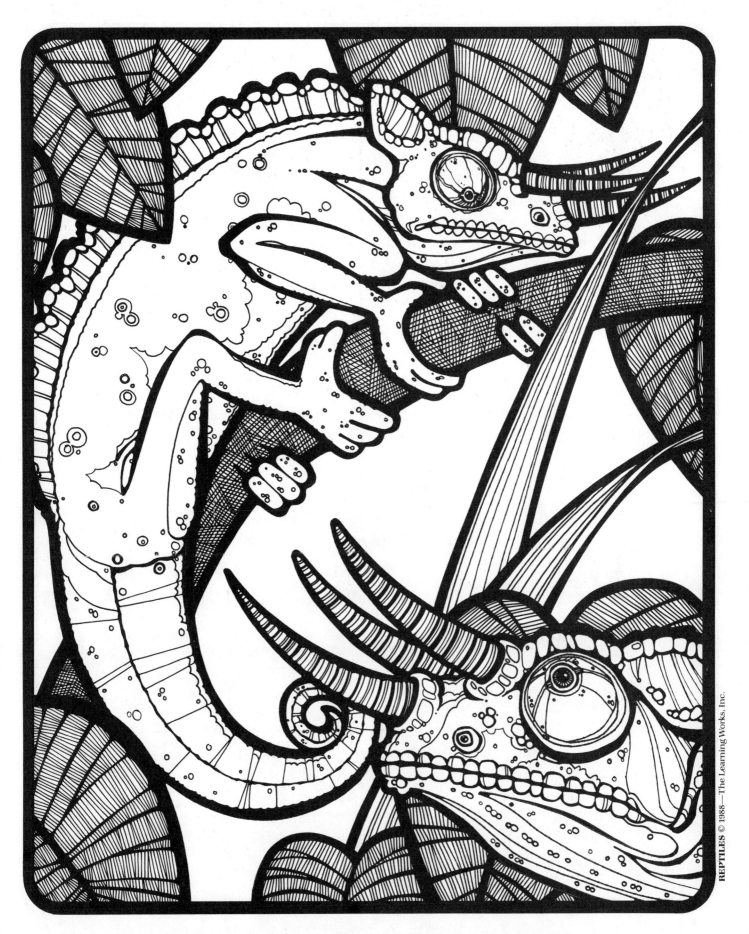

Jackson's Chameleon (*Chameleo jacksoni*)

Matamata

This strange South American turtle is designed for two things: hiding and eating. Its low, knobby shell, which may be covered with algae, can be easily concealed among the dead plants on a river bottom. Even when the matamata stretches its neck up to the water's surface to breathe, its loose, ragged skin makes it look like something dead and decaying. The matamata's tiny, beady eyes and wide mouth are hidden under its triangular head. This turtle catches its food by lying motionless underwater until fish come close, then suddenly opening its mouth, sucking in the fish, and swallowing them whole. Matamatas are poor swimmers and rarely leave the water.

Coloring Clues

The matamata is orange and rusty brown so that it easily blends with the dead leaves and mud on the bottoms of the rivers in which it lives.

Activity Safari

1. Many turtles have interesting names. Make a word search puzzle using some or all of the turtle names listed below.

bog	leopard	radiated
box	map	sawback
cooter	matamata	slider
diamondback	mud	snakeneck
four-eyed	musk	star
hawksbill	painted	stinkpot
hingeback		wood

2. To see how the matamata catches fish by suction, cut some quarter-inch-long pieces of rubber band and drop them into a tall glass of water. Cover the upper end of a straw with your index finger. Lower the straw into the water. Suck the rubber "fish" into the straw "turtle" by suddenly lifting your finger.

Matamata (*Chelys fimbriata*)

Moloch

The moloch lives in Australia's dry central deserts. This weird six-inch lizard is camouflaged by its coloration and protected by hundreds of sharp spines. Another name for the moloch is **thorny devil.** When frightened, the moloch tucks its head under its front legs and arches its back so that the two largest spines stick up.

The moloch eats ants. It sits near their holes or trails and snaps them up one at a time, eating as many as five thousand in one sitting. Such a meal could last a moloch for several weeks. Molochs can go for months without drinking. Dew collects on their heads and runs along tiny grooves in their spines and skin into their mouths.

The female moloch lays eggs in January. She slowly and carefully digs a sloping two-foot tunnel in soft sand. In this tunnel, she places up to ten inch-long eggs. Then she blocks the opening to the tunnel with sand. The baby molochs, each barely more than two inches long, emerge three months later.

Coloring Clues

The moloch is tan or orange with reddish brown spots.

Activity Safari

1. **Moloch** is the name of a savage, angry, ancient god. **Thorny devil** is another name that suggests fierceness. Yet this lizard is slow-moving and harmless. Can you think of a friendlier and more appropriate name for it?

2. How long would it take a moloch to eat two thousand ants at the rate of forty per minute?

3. The **echidna** is another strange, spiny, ant-eating Australian animal. Look up the echidna in an encyclopedia or book about mammals.

REPTILES © 1988—The Learning Works, Inc.

Moloch (*Moloch horridus*)

Nile Monitor

The Nile monitor is a powerful, active, aggressive lizard. Often more than six feet long, it has strong jaws, sharp claws, and a tail that can slash like a whip. The Nile monitor's appetite is enormous; its favorite foods are the eggs and young of Nile crocodiles. These monitors are excellent swimmers and can outrun a man. They live along rivers and like to lie on tree branches overhanging the water so they can dive and swim when danger threatens.

Female monitors lay eggs in termite nests, where the hard, dry mud keeps them safe and warm. The young emerge five months later, scrambling out in search of insects, snails, and frogs. They need no parental care.

Coloring Clues

Young Nile monitors, such as the one shown here, are brightly marked with black and yellow. Older specimens develop a brown or gray-green color.

Activity Safari

1. The range of the Nile monitor extends from Senegal to Somalia and from Egypt to South Africa. Locate these four countries on a map of Africa.

2. Make a bar graph comparing the length of the six-foot Nile monitor with the lengths of these other lizards.

banded tegu	4 feet	goanna	7 feet
common iguana	6 feet	komodo dragon	10 feet
Gila monster	2 feet	marine iguana	5 feet

3. Design a zoo enclosure for a pair of Nile monitors. Remember that they need warmth, sunlight, shelter, and water. What would be the best way to confine the animals without blocking the public's view of them?

Nile Monitor (*Varanus niloticus*)

Spectacled Caiman

Caimans are related to alligators and crocodiles, but are smaller and more aggressive than these other large reptiles. Spectacled caimans are about six feet long. They live in the rivers of Central and South America. Their name comes from the ridge between their eyes, which makes them appear to be wearing glasses.

Spectacled caimans feed on all kinds of animals, including amphibians, birds, fish, mammals, and other reptiles. In some areas, they cause problems by attacking livestock. Their main enemies are anacondas, jaguars, and people. Piranhas share the spectacled caimans' habitat but rarely attack them.

The female caiman lays her eggs in a mound of mud and plants. When her babies are ready to hatch, they make croaking noises. These sounds alert the mother, who uncovers the eggs. Unlike most female reptiles, the female caiman protects her offspring.

Coloring Clues

This caiman is golden tan. Its eyes are blue or gray.

Activity Safari

1. A caiman six feet and eight inches long was swallowed by an anaconda twenty-three feet and four inches long. How much longer than the caiman was the snake?

2. Young caimans are sometimes sold as pets under the name of "baby alligators." For what reasons would these animals *not* make good pets?

3. Many caimans live along the Amazon River in South America. Look up the length of this river in an atlas or an encyclopedia. Is it longer or shorter than the distance from Seattle, Washington, to Miami, Florida (2,650 miles)?

REPTILES © 1988—The Learning Works, Inc.

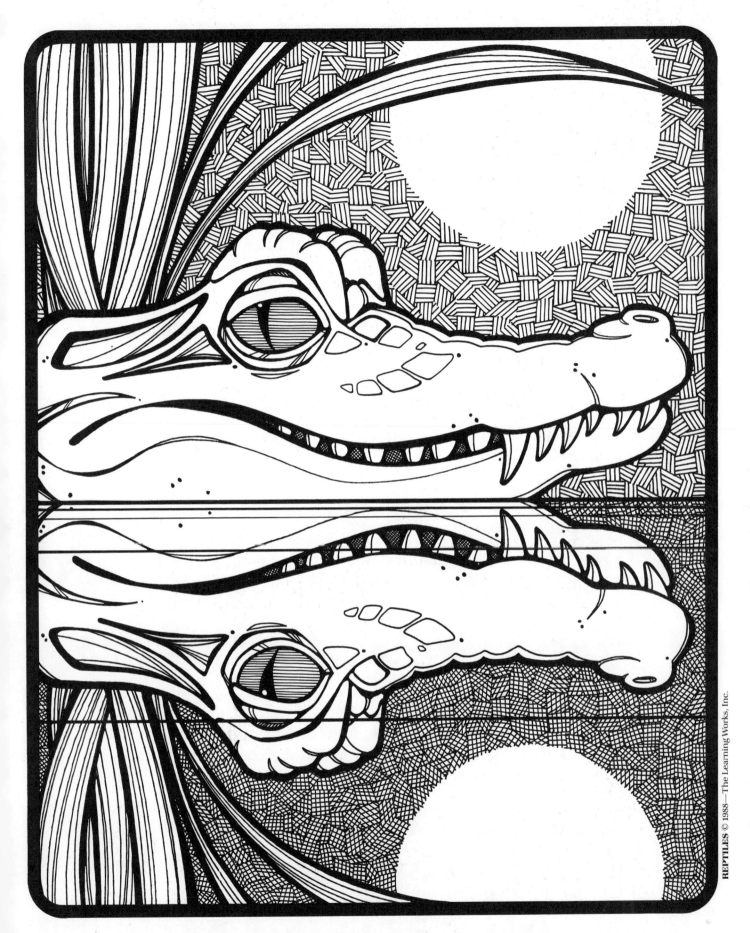

Spectacled Caiman (*Caiman crocodilus*)

Spiny Soft-Shelled Turtle

Spiny soft-shelled turtles are found in lakes and streams in many parts of the United States. Other soft-shelled turtles are found in Africa and Asia. The word *spiny* in this turtle's name refers to the short, scratchy spines on the back of its shell. These weird-looking turtles hide underwater, buried in mud and sand. To breathe, they stretch their long, flexible necks up to the surface of the water. Spiny soft-shelled turtles are capable swimmers and have little trouble catching crayfish and fish to eat. When captured, they defend themselves fiercely with their strong jaws and sharp claws. The maximum size for spiny soft-shelled turtles is fifteen inches. Among this particular species, females are larger than males.

Coloring Clues

The spiny soft-shelled turtle is tan with black and gray spots. Its eyes are yellow.

Activity Safari

1. One reason the soft-shelled turtle must be so aggressive is that it lacks a large, strong shell in which to hide when threatened. As you might gather from their name, snapping turtles are also very aggressive. Find a picture of a snapping turtle, and note the size of its shell.

2. Draw a cartoon strip in which a grouchy soft-shelled turtle tries to catch a sneaky fish.

3. The soft-shelled turtle's flattened body, dull color, and long, snorkel-like neck all help it live successfully at the bottom of ponds and streams. The animals listed below are well adapted for life on the ocean floor. Do some research to learn about one or more of them.

flounder   horseshoe crab   sand dollar   sting ray

Spiny Soft-Shelled Turtle (*Trionyx spiniferus*)

Reptile Facts

There are more than 2,000 species of snake. Only about 150 of them are venomous enough to be dangerous to people.

Snake-necked turtles have necks almost as long as their shells.

The largest reptile is the saltwater crocodile. It may weigh two tons and be more than twenty-five feet long.

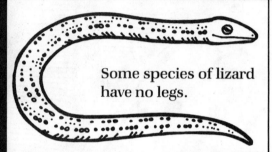

Some species of lizard have no legs.

The American alligator may live as long as fifty-six years.

The six-lined race runner lizard can zip along at a speed of eighteen miles per hour.

The snapping turtle uses its wormlike tongue to lure fishes into its mouth.

Snakes can swim.

There are about 3,000 species of lizard alive today.

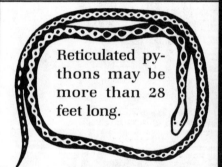

Reticulated pythons may be more than 28 feet long.

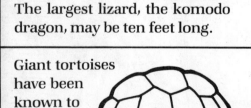

The largest lizard, the komodo dragon, may be ten feet long.

The fastest snake is the black mamba.

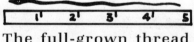

The full-grown thread snake may be less than five inches long.

Giant tortoises have been known to live for 150 years.

Some snakes "play dead" when they meet a person or other enemy.

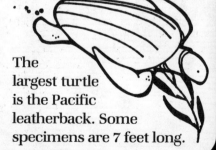

The largest turtle is the Pacific leatherback. Some specimens are 7 feet long.